Looking at . . . Diplodocus
A Dinosaur from the JURASSIC Period

Weekly Reader®
BOOKS

Published by arrangement with Gareth Stevens, Inc.
Newfield Publications is a federally registered trademark
of Newfield Publications, Inc. Weekly Reader is a federally
registered trademark of Weekly Reader Corporation.

Library of Congress Cataloging-in-Publication Data

Coleman, Graham, 1963-
    Looking at-- Diplodocus/written by Graham Coleman; illustrated by Tony Gibbons.
        p. cm. -- (The New dinosaur collection)
    Includes index.
    ISBN 0-8368-1084-8
    1. Diplodocus--Juvenile literature. [1. Diplodocus. 2. Dinosaurs.] I. Gibbons, Tony, ill.
II. Title. III. Series.
QE862.S3C64 1994
567.9'7--dc20   93-37054

This North American edition first published in 1994 by
Gareth Stevens Publishing
1555 North RiverCenter Drive, Suite 201
Milwaukee, Wisconsin 53212 USA

This U.S. edition © 1994 by Gareth Stevens, Inc. Created with original
© 1993 by Quartz Editorial Services, Premier House, 112 Station Road,
Edgware HA8 7AQ U.K.

Consultant: Dr. David Norman, Director of the Sedgwick Museum of Geology,
University of Cambridge, England.

Additional artwork by Clare Heronneau.

Printed in the United States of America

Weekly Reader Books Presents

Looking at . . .
Diplodocus
A Dinosaur from the JURASSIC Period

by Graham Coleman

Illustrated by Tony Gibbons

Gareth Stevens Publishing
MILWAUKEE

Contents

Introducing
Diplodocus

Diplodocus (DIP-LOD-OH-KUS) was one of the longest dinosaurs that ever lived. Its barrel-like body was balanced by a very long tail and a long, thin neck that ended in a tiny head.

Despite its great size, **Diplodocus** was a very light dinosaur that weighed about 10 tons. **Brachiosaurus** (BRACK-EE-OH-SAW-RUS), for example, weighed several times as much as **Diplodocus**, even though its body was not as long.

Diplodocus lived in what is now North America about 145 million years ago in Jurassic times. It fed only on plants and was therefore a herbivore.

When was it that **Diplodocus** was first discovered? Why was it so lightweight compared to other big dinosaurs? Did it live in water or on land?

Since its remains were first discovered in 1877, scientists have succeeded in finding out a great deal about **Diplodocus**.

Turn the pages that follow and discover what is now known about this fantastic dinosaur.

5

Long-necked dinosaur

Imagine yourself swept back in time to the age of the dinosaurs. You would have looked tiny standing next to the giant **Diplodocus**, and you would have had to stretch your neck to look up at it.

Diplodocus was as tall as a four-story building and as long as three buses. Most of its length consisted of its neck and tail.

6

The bones in its neck were light-weight but very strong. This made it easy for **Diplodocus** to raise and lower its head when eating.

Diplodocus's tail was its only real method of defense. It was used as a powerful weapon if another dinosaur was brave enough to launch an attack against this gigantic dinosaur.

The tail could have also been used to help **Diplodocus** keep its balance if it reared up on its back legs in order to eat from a very tall tree.

Early scientists thought **Diplodocus** lived in water. But evidence later showed this was not so.

The pressure of the surrounding water on its lungs would have made it impossible for **Diplodocus** to breathe in enough air to survive.

Even marshy ground would have presented problems for **Diplodocus**, since it would easily have sunk or gotten stuck. It would have preferred hard, dry ground to move across on its thick legs.

Because of its tremendous size, **Diplodocus** may seem very frightening. But it would never attack unless in self-defense.

Most of the toenails on its front feet were like hooves. But the first toe on each foot had claws that were also useful against predators.

Scientists have marveled at the amount of pressure that would have been necessary to pump **Diplodocus**'s blood all the way from its heart around such a huge body — particularly up its long neck to its brain!

Lightweight skeleton

Diplodocus was a **Sauropod** (SOAR-OH-POD). This group of huge land animals got its name, meaning "reptile feet," from the five-toed feet that were very much like those of a reptile.

But unlike many other large dinosaurs, **Diplodocus**'s bones were very lightweight.

This is because many of the bones were hollow.

Diplodocus's skull was very small for such a large animal. Since it had a very small brain, about the same size as a cat's, scientists do not think **Diplodocus** could have been a very intelligent dinosaur.

Its teeth were small and thin, and they were all bunched together at the front of its mouth. When they wore down, it is possible that new ones grew back in their place.

Diplodocus had small eyes that were placed near the back of its head. Strangely, this giant creature had nostrils on top of its head.

Its ribs were very long, and they protected its big chest and belly. The feet were short, and there were five toes on each.

Diplodocus had great strength in its tail, which had 70 bones, but there were only 15 in its neck and 10 in its back. The secret of this dinosaur's power lay in the strong bones in its haunches.

How, then, did **Diplodocus** manage to keep its tremendously long neck suspended in the air? The answer is that it had powerful muscles and tendons to help with this. These worked a bit like a mechanical crane.

Scientists believe its tail was probably often held off the ground as it plodded along, rather than being dragged around all the time. Notice how the tail gets narrower and narrower toward its very end.

At the tip, this whiplike tail was only as wide as your little finger. **Diplodocus**'s skeleton may have been very light, but its legs were nevertheless very strong, like those of today's elephants. It also had great power in its back muscles.

Diplodocus may have even been able to support its body weight on just one of these pillarlike legs. So it had no trouble at all when rearing up on its two back legs to reach and nibble on leaves at the top of the very tallest trees.

Diplodocus

Diplodocus was one of the dinosaurs discovered during the "Bone Wars" of the last century. Two American paleontologists (scientists who study the remains of living creatures), Edward Cope and Othniel C. Marsh, were bitter rivals.

They both had teams of men working for them, digging for dinosaur bones across the United States. Both men competed to find the best dinosaur skeletons, and their teams often fought over remains, as you can see in the picture.

In 1877, some particularly interesting bones were found by one of Marsh's men.

This famous scientist named the creature from which the bones came *Diplodocus*, which means "double beam," after an unusual bone formation in its body.

discovered

A few years later, a famous American businessman, Andrew Carnegie, decided he wanted a big dinosaur for his new museum in Philadelphia, Pennsylvania. Before long, he was presented with a huge **Diplodocus** skeleton.

Soon everyone had heard about Carnegie's dinosaur. The King of England, Edward VII, even asked for a life-size model to be made by Carnegie's museum. The model was made and sent to London's Natural History Museum. It took two years to construct.

Over the next few years, **Diplodocus** proved so popular that copies were sent to museums all around the world!

Today, these skeletons of **Diplodocus** and other dinosaur giants are as popular as ever.

In Late Jurassic times

In **Diplodocus**'s day, the weather was very warm and damp all year round. This meant plants had ideal growing conditions. This was good for **Diplodocus** because it spent most of its time looking for plants to eat.

Herds of these giant dinosaurs lumbered across the landscape, crushing the ferns that grew on the ground.

Smaller dinosaurs, such as **Coelurus** (SEEL-OO-RUS), had to be quick on their feet to avoid getting crushed by a herd of **Diplodocus**.

Diplodocus was a peaceful animal but not very nimble or intelligent, so it had to watch out for predators.

13

Life with Diplodocus

Diplodocus was a plant-eating dinosaur. It used its long neck to reach up into the trees and bite off juicy leaves.

Diplodocus had pencil-like teeth at the front of its mouth. Because of the shape of its teeth, **Diplodocus** could not chew its food easily.

14

However, it probably swallowed pebbles or tiny stones and used these to grind food into small pieces that it could then digest.

Herds of **Diplodocus** traveled across the conifer forests of the Jurassic landscape, looking for trees and other plants to eat.

Diplodocus could eat from tall trees that other dinosaurs could not reach. When a **Diplodocus** herd had stripped one part of the forest, it then moved on to find new feeding grounds.

For such huge dinosaurs, it was always time to eat.

Look out!

It was late afternoon on a hot Jurassic day. A herd of **Diplodocus** was moving slowly through the forests. Occasionally, one of these giant dinosaurs stopped to nibble at the tops of the most tasty-looking trees.

But they were not the only hungry dinosaurs around.

As the **Diplodocus** moved on, they did not realize they were getting nearer and nearer to the territory of **Allosaurus** (AL-OH-SAW-RUS).

These vicious meat-eating dinosaurs weren't as big as **Diplodocus**.

But they were built for fighting. Even so, attacking a herd of **Diplodocus** was no easy matter.

16

An **Allosaurus** hid behind a group of trees and waited until the last **Diplodocus** had passed. It had noticed that the last **Diplodocus** in the herd was an old one. The old dinosaur lumbered along slowly, lagging behind the more energetic, younger ones. Thirsty, it stopped at a lake and bent its head to drink, unaware of what was about to happen.

But although it was old, it was not going to give up without a fight.

Allosaurus lost its grasp on **Diplodocus**'s back and fell to the ground. But it was soon back on its feet and ready for another lunge. It had not reckoned on the mighty force of **Diplodocus**'s tail, however. The larger dinosaur summoned all its energy and swung its tail at **Allosaurus**. The meat-eater felt a crushing blow to its body.

Suddenly, the **Allosaurus** leapt out from behind the trees! Viciously, it jumped on the **Diplodocus**'s back, sinking its sharp teeth into its skin. **Diplodocus** was taken by surprise and knocked off balance.

Again, it fell to the ground. But this time it did not get up.

Through the eyes

Have you ever wondered what the world must have looked like through the eyes of a gigantic dinosaur? **Diplodocus**'s eyes were about 33 feet (10 m) above the ground and set on either side of its head.

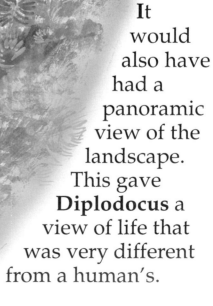

So, like many animals today, **Diplodocus** saw two pictures of what lay ahead.

It would also have had a panoramic view of the landscape. This gave **Diplodocus** a view of life that was very different from a human's.

# of Diplodocus

Like modern reptiles, dinosaurs probably saw the world in color.

Modern reptiles also have eyes that can see very clearly in the nighttime as well as during the day. **Diplodocus** may also have been able to see in the dark.

And as its eyes were set far back on its head, it was probably not easy for another dinosaur to creep up without being seen by **Diplodocus**.

Diplodocus and cousins

Diplodocus (1) gave its name to the group of dinosaurs to which it belongs — the **Diplodocids**. All the **Diplodocids** had long necks and tails, pillarlike legs, and small heads. These dinosaurs were large plant-eaters and lived all over the world. They flourished at the end of the Jurassic Period, between 150 and 135 million years ago. All the **Diplodocids** were **Sauropods**.

Barosaurus (<u>BAH</u>-RO-<u>SAW</u>-RUS) **(4)**, whose name means "heavy reptile," grew to 88 feet (27 m) in length, about the same size as its relative, **Diplodocus**. Remains of **Barosaurus** have been found in the western United States and in Tanzania, Africa. This shows that the continents of North America and Africa were once linked and that dinosaurs wandered across huge land masses.

3

Mamenchisaurus (MA-<u>MENCH</u>-EE-<u>SAW</u>-RUS) **(3)** was another enormous **Sauropod**. It is named after the Mamenchin region of China where it was found. It is believed to have had the longest neck of any creature ever to have lived on Earth. Its neck was 36 feet (11 m) long — that's even longer than a bus — and made up half of **Mamenchisaurus**'s entire length.

Apatosaurus (A-<u>PAT</u>-OH-<u>SAW</u>-RUS) **(2)** is the best known of **Diplodocus**'s relatives. *Apatosaurus* is the scientific name for the dinosaur that was, at one time, commonly known as *Brontosaurus* (<u>BRON</u>-TOE-<u>SAW</u>-RUS).

The name *Apatosaurus* had been given first, so the name *Brontosaurus* was dropped. **Apatosaurus** was heavier than **Diplodocus** but not as long. Its name means "deceptive reptile."

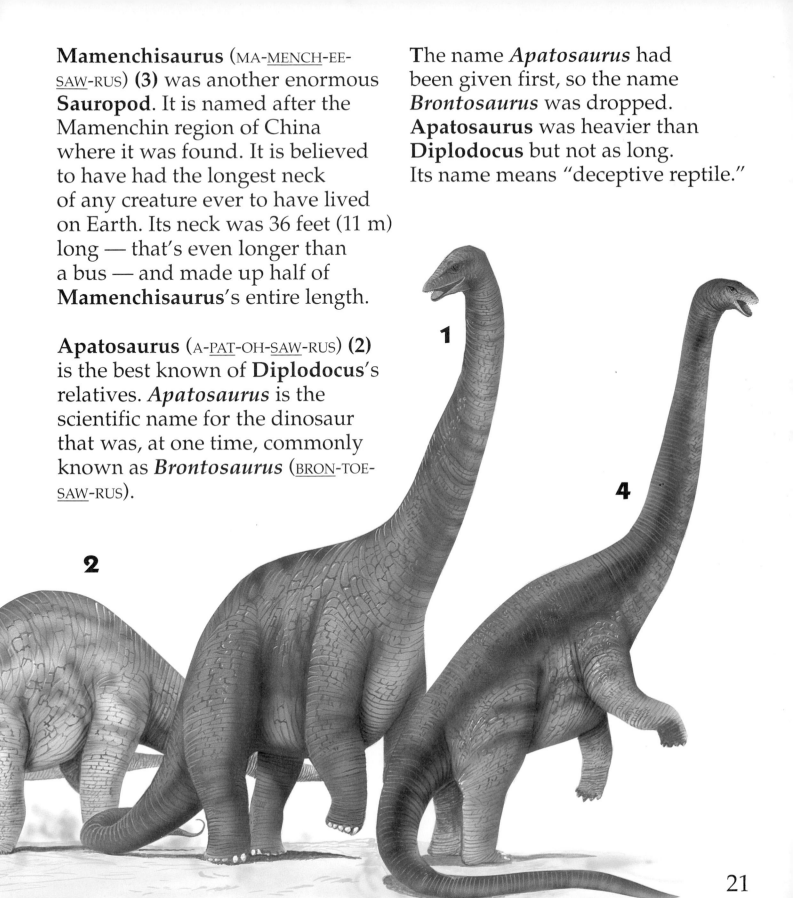

Diplodocus data

Diplodocus belonged to a group of dinosaurs called **Sauropods**. They were large plant-eaters with long necks and tails. Although **Diplodocus** was not a heavy dinosaur compared to some of the other **Sauropods** — **Apatosaurus**, for example — it was still an enormous creature and needed sturdy feet to support its body.

Like other large plant-eaters, **Diplodocus** had such a large stomach that if it had walked on its back legs only, it might have toppled over!

Some scientists, however, believe that **Diplodocus** could have reared up on its two back legs to reach the tallest trees. Then it would have rested its tail on the ground and propped itself against the trunk of the tree with its front legs. This way it could be comfortable enough to eat.

Broad feet

Diplodocus's feet were short and broad. Each foot had five short, strong toes. Scientists also think **Diplodocus** may have had claws on two of its back toes and one claw on its front toes. Apart from the claws, **Diplodocus**'s feet were very similar to those of an elephant.

Slender neck

Diplodocus's long, thin neck contained 15 hollow bones. **Diplodocus** could swing its neck up and down and use its tail as a balance.

Double beam

Diplodocus gets its name, which means "double beam," from an unusual feature of its backbone. It had pairs of small bones below the backbone with pieces that ran forward as well as backward, like double beams.

Bony tail

Diplodocus's long, thin, whiplike tail had 70 bones in it, which made it an extremely powerful weapon against predators.

Small head

Diplodocus had a small head for such an enormous creature. Its eyes were on either side of its head, and it had thin teeth at the front of its mouth. Its nostrils were positioned on top of its head. At the back of the skull was a small case for this huge animal's tiny brain.

GLOSSARY

conifers — woody shrubs or trees that bear their seeds in cones.

continents — the major land masses of Earth. Europe, Africa, Asia, Australia, North America, South America, and Antarctica are continents.

haunches — the hip, buttocks, and thigh area of animals and humans.

herbivores — plant-eating animals.

herd — a group of animals that travels together.

hoof (hooves) — a strong covering of horn that protects the feet of certain animals.

predators — animals that kill other animals for food.

remains — a dead body or corpse.

reptiles — cold-blooded animals that have hornlike or scaly skin.

skeleton — the bony framework of a body.

INDEX